# A HOUSE IN MAINE

## NINA CAMPBELL

# A HOUSE
# IN MAINE

## NINA CAMPBELL

Giles Kime
Photography by Paul Raeside

*RIZZOLI*
NEW YORK

New York Paris London Milan

# CONTENTS

———————

# INTRODUCTION

When, at the turn of the last century, a couple built a simple cottage among towering spruce trees and verdant ferns that overlooked a secluded bay off the coast of Maine, they had no inkling that they were creating a legacy that would become central to the lives of several generations of their family. With successive incremental additions it grew into a Federal-style manse at the heart of a small seaside estate. Along with its surrounding three hundred acres, this is a magical place where their children, grandchildren, and great-grandchildren have experienced holidays that couldn't be further removed from their lives in the city. These were summers when the foundations for lifelong friendships were established beneath the spreading branches of the maple that offered shade to the house and garden.

More than a century later, their great-grandson and his wife met the legendary English interior designer Nina Campbell in Nassau, in the Bahamas. They were familiar with Campbell's role as the designer of Annabel's, the private members' club in London established in the 1960s that was popular with the Rolling Stones, Diana Ross, and Ella Fitzgerald. The couple had a hunch that she was the person to create a sociable new incarnation of the house for their family and future generations to enjoy. They felt it was time for the house to evolve while remaining true to its past. For him, this was always a place that the family had loved to share—and parties at the house, in the garden, and down at the dock were the perfect way to do so. It was this role that was about to move center stage in the next iteration of their summer home.

But before he could enlist Campbell's help, the decision had to be made about the beloved maple tree that had begun to overwhelm the house. Should they move the house or move the tree? Such was its totemic presence in their lives, it was a question that barely needed to be asked; New York architects Ferguson & Shamamian were asked to move the house, incorporating some of the existing structure and re-creating it in the same spirit while making changes inside and out that would provide the perfect setting for entertaining and family life in the twenty-first century. With a dedicated party villa (known as the Playhouse), bowling alley, pool house, and tennis pavilion as well as accommodation for family and friends dreamed up by the world-famous designer, this exciting project established the property as a place for fun and relaxation for generations to come.

In an era when lives have become progressively more transitory, the bond between successive generations of the family and this plot of land speaks volumes about a subject that is rarely addressed in discussions of interior design and architecture; the magnetic draw of homes with a sense of place and also those imbued with memories of people and experiences. Of course, the look and shape of our residences are governed by many things—not least by the way that spaces are configured and the colors, light, and things that fill them—but it is the emotional draw that dominates all of these variables and ultimately

determines their importance in our lives. This is perhaps the magic of this secluded inlet on America's Atlantic coast, which has been sympathetically and deftly reinvented for life today by weaving together the most important elements of past and present, whether by maintaining the position of a much-loved veranda but transforming it with adjustments to scale or bringing new life to a much-loved bench where generations have enjoyed the panoramic sea views.

Through the centuries, our approach to old buildings has been polarized between the shock and awe of the bulldozer and the gentle touch of the restorer. From the single-minded vision of Baron Haussmann, whose transformation of France's capital rode roughshod over swaths of medieval Paris, to the work of Italian architect Carlo Scarpa, whose architectural interventions of many of the Veneto's most iconic buildings were informed by the region's past, it is a distinction that has shaped the way we live. But as this project demonstrates, there is a middle way that is increasingly being followed by architects and interior designers, particularly those

ABOVE: Nina Campbell first met the owners of the Maine property in Nassau, in the Bahamas. After taking on the project, Campbell made numerous visits to the state before, during, and after construction. As well as conceiving the interiors here, she also worked on the decoration of the couple's Manhattan apartment.

who have recognized that a respect for the past and a desire for modern comforts aren't mutually exclusive. The combined skill, experience, and instinct of Nina Campbell—Britain's foremost interior designer, with over fifty years at the top of her game—and Ferguson & Shamamian's innate understanding of the scale, proportion, and detail that are the foundation of classic architecture have been the secrets to the success of this project.

Mark Ferguson and Oscar Shamamian launched their own practice in 1988, after meeting when they both worked for decorator Albert Hadley—who was also a friend of Campbell's. Together, they have created some of America's most distinctive homes grounded in a quiet classicism that blends the best of old and new and that celebrates the beauty of both materials and time-honored craftsmanship. They have demonstrated the benefits of taking a holistic approach to their projects, from urban apartments to mountain retreats, the magic of which is built on a foundation of collaborative relationships with interior designers, landscape designers, builders, and craftspeople. The most important relationships, however, are with their clients whose initial hopes and aspirations are brought to life in a way they could never have dreamed possible.

The foundation for Nina Campbell's lifetime of projects has been not only on collaboration but also on comfort. Her work ranges from historic English houses completed under the guidance of renowned designer John Fowler to projects as diverse as John Nash–designed Regency-era Belgravia town houses and Kensington apartments to a German schloss and, for a decorator show house, the reimagining of the bedroom of ill-fated Ned Doheny in the celebrated 1920s Greystone Mansion in Los Angeles. Yet in her hands, comfort is more than just physical, it is also aesthetic and emotional; color and pattern blend seamlessly and with familiarity, whether she is using clients' existing pieces or bringing in new and distinctive acquisitions that reflect her clients' own tastes and interests, resulting in rooms that feel as if they were made distinctly for the inhabitants. It is these elements that bring as much comfort as a deeply upholstered chair. Anyone who has studied the succession of homes that Nina Campbell created for her growing family in South Kensington and Chelsea in the 1980s and '90s will see the same treasured pieces of furniture and lighting being used again and again, sometimes in a new guise or with proportions adjusted for each new setting. It is this understanding of what it takes to create environments with soul that is at the heart of the interiors she has created in this unique house by the sea.

PRECEDING SPREADS & OPPOSITE: The property is separated from the outside world both by the sea and by dense woodland, predominantly spruce that in places was cleared to create paths as well as an area for clay pigeon shooting. Such native varieties as sweet gale, winterberry, and bayberry were planted to soften the transition between domestic areas of the estate and the wild. An early farm building was restored to maintain a link to the area's agrarian past.

# THE MAIN HOUSE

ABOVE & OPPOSITE: The simple, classically inspired entrance to the main house keeps the spirit of the original residence that stood here for over a century. The discreet architectural detailing continues in the entrance hall where a curlicue motif on the staircase is typical of the measured approach of the New York architecture firm Ferguson & Shamamian.

There are a few well-trodden options open to anyone lucky enough to take possession of a tired but much-loved family house. One is to tenderly bring it into the present day, reinventing spaces intended for a different way of life. The other is to knock it down and start from scratch with modified footprint, ceiling heights, and appearance to make it workable for a new era. Or, of course, it can be left in a state of gradual decay for another generation to address.

There's also another path, less traveled, that involves building a new house that embodies the spirit of the old with many of the same treasured elements, the same access to light, and the same orientation to harness a distinctive sense of place that evokes generations of memories of people and experiences. That, in essence, is the subject of this book: a property with a house that has been rebuilt in almost exactly the same location as its predecessor and that combines the emotional strands of the past with the necessities of the future. Into the warp and weft are woven other elements, not least the tastes and personalities of the owners as well as the materials and artisanal traditions of the local area.

Weaving is a complex art, requiring a mix of skill, experience, an understanding of materials, and an instinctive eye for color, pattern, and texture—attributes that made Nina Campbell the perfect person to work

with Ferguson & Shamamian on a project with a greater range of nuances than most and one that would involve an intimate working relationship with the clients. While the body of the house was moved, its elevation when seen from the sea is similar in appearance and proportion with much of the mass of the building extended to the land side. Some of the spaces have the same outlook and orientation but have simply evolved. On the shaded veranda, where doors fully retract to expose the inside to the outside, the connection with the past is enhanced by the sofa that stills sits, restored and reupholstered, in the same position that it has had for decades.

The masterstroke in the conception of the house—as it is in all Ferguson & Shamamian's projects—was to create a new house with spaces and proportions that look as though they have been there forever, but which conceal services that are carefully considered, beautifully engineered, and truly state of the art. Such architectural details as handsome fitted cupboards with lattice glazing, shallow arches, and discreet plaster detailing add a layer of interest that replaces the sense of permanence in the previous structure.

Against this backdrop another layer was added by Campbell and her team. So often in new-build houses, the role of decoration is to overcome the clinical atmosphere and austere lines that can be their dominant feature. Here, the scene had been set by the

OPPOSITE: On a wall of the central stairway, decorative artist Dean Barger painted landscape scenes with birch trees and ferns onto a Phillip Jeffries grasscloth wallcovering. The original entrance hall featured painted murals that were preserved and framed, and are now on display in an upstairs hallway.

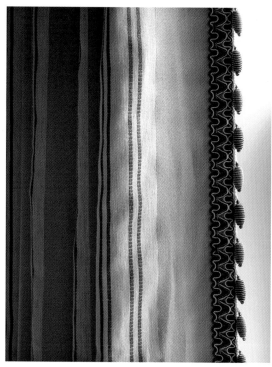

PRECEDING SPREAD, ABOVE & OPPOSITE: The main sitting room occupies a similar location as the sitting room of the original house. The floor is painted in a simple gray-and-white checkerboard pattern and is topped with a large, room-size rush mat. The embroidered stools—with depictions of the clients' dogs—are from Tapisserie in London.

architecture and simply needed the addition of comfort and a light touch that would re-establish it at the latest iteration of the family home. In this respect, Campbell was helped by the owners' request to indulge their love of purple, lilac, mauve, and lavender. It's a palette that pervades but doesn't overwhelm and that mixes well with such neutral hues as taupes, grays, and silver. While not rigidly imposed, it creates a sense of coherence as one moves from room to room and from floor to floor.

The clients' request for a tranquil color scheme also set the course for the overall feel of the scheme. So often designers create schemes for seaside residences that take their cues from the surrounding landscape, but these interiors have a look that, while sympathetic to the geography, have an energy that is very much their own. They also address the fact that much of the appeal of this house is the views, and the spare, pared-back approach ensures that there isn't too much that will distract from the glorious natural light. The windows, like the internal doors, are as tall as possible to maximize the impact of the setting while also framing the vistas beautifully.

The main sitting room is Nina Campbell at her most delicate, with a look and feel that are enhanced further by a floor painted in a large checkerboard pattern in white and gray. On top is a room-size rug woven in rush, an English tradition that dates to the Anglo-Saxon period and that does much to soften the appearance of rooms while also absorbing sound.

Considered and comfortable furniture plans are one of the hallmarks of Campbell's work; the main

RIGHT & FOLLOWING SPREAD: The porch, leading from both the sitting room and the dining room, also featured in the original house and has been made slightly wider. The wall lights are from Niermann Weeks. The clients' existing octagonal center table was repainted by Campbell's team.

32

The Gardens of Russell Page

seating area is centered on a set of four steel-and-glass tables while the second focuses on an oval glass-topped table, pieces that do not overwhelm their surroundings. A pair of painted console tables, each with a pier glass above, creates symmetry and blends seamlessly with the setting.

Having set the scene with a mixture of soft colors—punctuated with refined touches such as decorative wall sconces, rattan chairs, and mirrors—the contemplative hues are continued throughout the ground floor and the principal bedroom suites. The genius of the architects' work is their ability to blend traditional domestic architecture with the demands of the twenty-first century. Throughout the different floors and wings of the building, the proportions and architectural detail blend to create a look that is true to the original building without ever descending into pastiche. Nor is there any sense that retaining any existing elements of this much-loved house has compromised the design of the remodeled structure. The artful balance of old and new is epitomized by the display of framed fragments of a mural depicting rural scenes that were saved from the entrance hall of the former house and hung so that they captured the spirit of the place in its past incarnation.

ABOVE, OPPOSITE & FOLLOWING SPREAD: One of the many joys of this reinvented house is its connection with the coastal setting, which is significantly enhanced by the size and proportions of the windows. The windows of the porch recede into the floor to create a seamless join between the indoors and out. Curtains in a semitransparent voile shield the space from strong sunlight.

PRECEDING SPREAD: The study, with touches of lavender and olive green, preserves many of the architectural features of the original house. ABOVE: Campbell has decorated the walls of the elevator with botanical prints featuring different varieties of fern, which are such an important feature of the grounds that surround the property. OPPOSITE: A view from the dining room to the entrance hall. FOLLOWING SPREAD: Above the dining table is a hanging light that Campbell had made from several wall sconces, creating an impression of sea creatures.

PRECEDING SPREADS: In the dining room, against a subtle palette of colors, the addition of purple glass, table linens, and flowers brings the space to life. OPPOSITE: One of the most striking of Campbell's recent designs is Cathay Parade, which features on the dining room curtains. ABOVE: Replicas of antique Chinese figures were made for the space and painted by Alice Clark to coordinate with Campbell's fabric.

ABOVE: Even compact spaces are layered with detail, in particular mirrored items. Wall sconces and a pair of Lalique taps lend a luxurious feel to the washstand in one of the downstairs bathrooms. OPPOSITE: The gong hanging from the beak of a decorative eagle head is used to summon guests to meals. A shaped leading edge gives a discreetly decorative touch to the curtains.

ABOVE & OPPOSITE: Between the dining room and the kitchen is a pantry that is used principally for the storage of extensive collections of china. Both Campbell and her client have acquired the many services used for entertaining in the dining room and around the property. The cabinetry was fitted by kitchen specialist Christopher Peacock.

OPPOSITE & ABOVE: The china with a chicken motif is from Gien, the notable French ceramics manufacturer founded in the Loire Valley in 1821 by Englishman Thomas Hall. At an antiques fair Campbell found the set of green tableware, which the clients use when serving fish stew.

ABOVE: A specially commissioned coffee and tea service features lizards engaged in sporting activities that take place at the property. OPPOSITE: This project was a true meeting of minds; Campbell and her clients shared many aesthetic passions, including tableware and certain colors, in particular the lilac, mauve, and purple that appear throughout the house and ancillary buildings.

ABOVE & OPPOSITE: The family room is another of the spaces where lilac and purple feature. On the sofa are cushions in Campbell's Barbary Toile, specially printed on linen. Lucy Jane Cope painted motifs from the latter on the shades of the wall sconces. The garden room beyond this space has a tented ceiling.

ABOVE & OPPOSITE: The garden room is yet another space in the house that has been furnished to provide space for relaxation, in this case for unrushed breakfasts with a coastal view. The scheme is deliberately muted, with color limited to a few accessories such as the vibrant glass candlesticks. FOLLOWING SPREAD: Details of the comfortable family room and garden room.

ABOVE & OPPOSITE: A mix of vintage wicker and playful ceramics adds a relaxed feel to the spaces adjacent to the back porch while the framed navigation chart is a reminder of the area's maritime past. The boarded walls and ceiling, along with the stone floors, lend a functional feeling to this area of the house.

OPPOSITE & ABOVE: While the interiors of the house were being planned, a New York antiques dealer contacted Campbell's client to let her know that he still had a set of half columns that she had purchased years earlier. It was decided that they would add a handsome connection between the main floor's central stair hall and the landing at the top of the stairs.

PRECEDING SPREAD & OPPOSITE: An arrangement of exquisite porcelain-and-painted-copper flowers by Vladimir Kanevsky—including representations of foxglove, lily of the valley, and hydrangea—brings the garden to the upstairs stair hall. ABOVE: A fern sconce alludes to a common feature of the landscape.

ABOVE & OPPOSITE: The principal bedroom of the house is lent a cosseting feel with heavy curtains, pelmets, and roman blinds—all in Jay Flower from Jane Churchill—and a four-poster with draperies. The bed's discreet metal frame creates a much lighter feel than a traditional design, which can dominate the space.

OPPOSITE & ABOVE: The writing desk has been painted with a simple pattern that echoes the design of the curtains. The wall color unifies the textiles used in the upholstery of the corner sofa and ottoman as well as on the shades of the standing lamps.

ABOVE & OPPOSITE: A scalloped pelmet at the window, beautifully crafted joinery, tiled floor, and ceiling papered with a simple graphic pattern give this bathroom and dressing room a discreetly luxurious feel. Necklaces hang from small tailor's dummies atop a mirrored chest of drawers from the 1930s. The top of the wall paneling serves as a ledge for the display of plates, photography, and treasured objects.

ABOVE & OPPOSITE: This small upstairs sitting room is another example of how the property is more than just a summer house. Such intimate spaces as this one are ideal for the beginning and end of the season. The shelves to the right of the fireplace serve as a display area for a collection of opaline boxes, many of them from Guinevere Antiques in London.

OPPOSITE & ABOVE: One of the many highlights of the house is a collection of fragments of a mural that were framed at the well-known Manhattan firm J. Pocker and installed in an upstairs hallway. The scenic decoration is an important feature for generations of family members and the one that does the most to connect the reinvented house to its past.

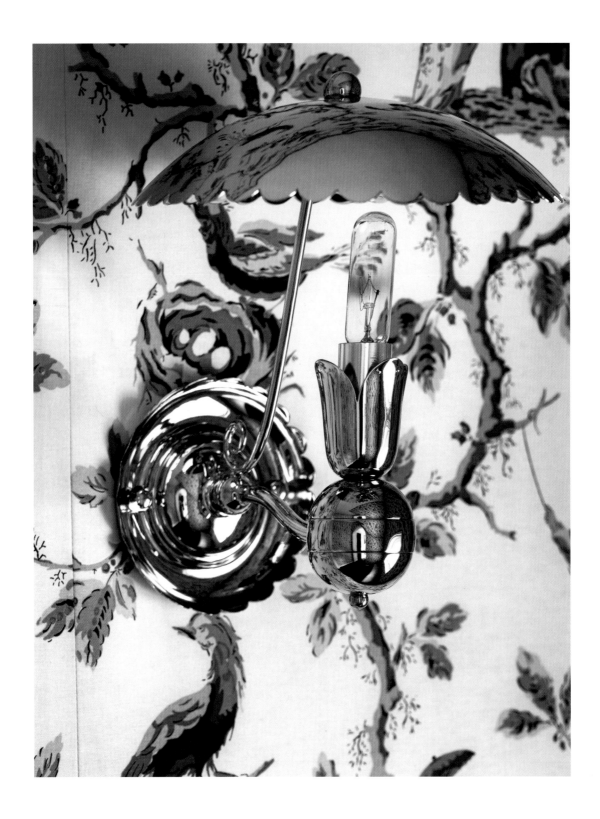

ABOVE & OPPOSITE: A niche that might have been what interior designers refer to as dead space—comprising little more than a small fan window and a pitched ceiling—has been brought to life with a blanket box in fabric from the Guy Goodfellow Collection and wallcovering in a chinoiserie fabric from Pierre Frey.

PRECEDING SPREAD, ABOVE & OPPOSITE: The pared-back bedroom suite of the clients' son is furnished with simple antique pieces that subtly evoke a period atmosphere. In the bathroom, a bespoke double vanity makes the most of all the available space, and small-format tiles feel cool underfoot.

ABOVE: Attention to detail is one of the hallmarks of Campbell's work. Three types of lighting—a picture light, a wall sconce, and a table lamp—create a layered illumination scheme. A built-in laundry hamper contains a linen bag embroidered with the name of the room.
OPPOSITE: The walls of the shower are lined in a simple graphic mosaic pattern by Waterworks.

ABOVE & OPPOSITE: The daughter's bedroom combines the homeowners' favorite lavender tones with pale blue—
as seen in the Quadrille fabric used on the pair of chairs, the ottoman, and the slipper chair in the bathroom.
Bedposts in a bobbin design lend the space a whimsical feel while a Tai Ping carpet adds luxury underfoot.
A pair of lights from the historic Parisian lighting manufacturer Baguès flanks the painting. The chest of drawers
is a favorite piece of furniture from the original house. FOLLOWING SPREAD: A fabric-lined alcove bed
adds extra sleeping accommodation in an adjoining room. The bathroom features a freestanding lavender tub.

ABOVE & OPPOSITE: In a guest bedroom suite, Campbell's Suzhou pattern, named after a Chinese garden city, lends a floral atmosphere to the curtained windows and the walls of a passageway. On the chair, the fabric has been quilted, piped, and gathered to add an extra level of luxury.

PRECEDING SPREAD: Illuminated floats from lobster pots are joined together with a specialized rope system and bring light to several floors of a back stairway. The carpet is from Pierre Frey. OPPOSITE & ABOVE: The bunk beds have curtains in a bespoke design—with motifs befitting a seaside house in Maine—from Chelsea Textiles.

ABOVE & OPPOSITE: The striking nautical theme of this bathroom includes a
bathtub fitted with a pair of portholes from the Water Monopoly, the London
specialist for Victorian and Edwardian bathrooms. FOLLOWING SPREAD: A striped
mattress with bolsters creates a comfortable window seat in a guest bedroom.

# THE POOL HOUSE

It's easy to forget that every interior, like every book, started with a blank sheet. The more distinct and more confident the style, the more convincing the illusion that somehow it was always there. New buildings create the greatest challenge, offering little in the way of visual cues other than their setting, and often it's the job of the decorator to find something that will act as a catalyst—a painting perhaps, a much-loved rug, or a favorite piece of furniture. In the pool house, items of furniture from another of the clients' residences in a distinctive large-scale blue-and-white pattern acted as inspiration for the decoration of the entire building. The classic combination is what binds this succession of spaces together, guiding the choice of everything from the bed linen to the color of door frames and banisters. The result? A relaxed scheme that is perfectly pitched for both its purpose and setting.

The relaxed, poolside setting of the main room is enhanced by such playful elements as the large-scale models of cans of sardines, crabmeat, and caviar. If interior design has the capacity to make guests feel relaxed, this space is a manifestation of that intention. The sitting room at the rear of the house is painted a deep blue that is in tune with the color schemes in the rest of the building—all creating a mood that is rich and cosseting. The room is also

lent significant charm by the family's large collection of model boats.

Upstairs, one guest room and adjoining bathroom in the eaves have a warm, intimate feel, with decoration that is classic Nina Campbell and that continues to play on the central theme of blue and white that dominates the rooms below. In the other bedroom suite is a red-and-white decorative scheme that is in dramatic contrast to the coherent approach in the rest of the house.

The descriptive name of the building is something of a misnomer; while it's a base from which to enjoy swimming, it also serves as yet another venue for entertaining and accommodating friends and family. It is rare during a stay at this property to ever dine in the same location more than once; there are settings for lunches, dinners, and impromptu cocktail parties everywhere, and this is one of them. At the pool house, drinks are dispensed from a long, freestanding bar that creates a welcoming atmosphere, and, when opened, doors in the main room recede fully to create a seamless connection between indoors and out. Throughout the property and the ancillary buildings, there are spaces that recognize that this is more than just a residence for high summer. While Maine has many extremes of weather, particularly in the winter, the property is the setting for family events and holidays from Easter through to Thanksgiving.

PRECEDING SPREAD & OPPOSITE: Most of the rooms in the pool house have a Mediterranean-style simplicity with a striking blue-and-white color palette. The boarded walls and pale linen curtains create a calm, recessive backdrop.

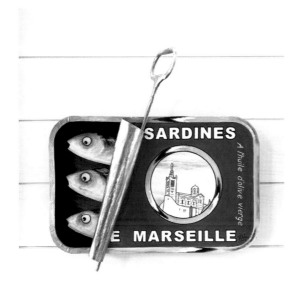

OPPOSITE & ABOVE: The mood in the pool house is relaxed and playful, a feeling enhanced by artwork based on such domestic items as overscale cans of sardines and caviar as well as glassware decorated with fish motifs. A fabric border adds a tailored decorative touch to a curtain.

OPPOSITE & ABOVE: Different shades of blue dominate the succession of spaces including the main living area and kitchen. A pair of overscale bulkhead lights hangs over the island bar, enhancing the nautical feel. Artwork in the shape of a whale adds a playful touch.

ABOVE & OPPOSITE: In some rooms, a moodier palette ensures that there are cozy spaces where guests can spend time on cooler days. The armchair is upholstered in Dianthus chintz from London-based Soane. The oval board with carved whales is a piece from the original house. The room is also home to a collection of ship models—some old, and some recent additions.

OPPOSITE & ABOVE: Although these spaces have a pared-back feel, they are rich in the details that characterize Campbell's work. A recurring feature in this project is the use of fabric borders, which offer a simple way to add a decorative touch to curtains and blinds in plain fabrics.

119

OPPOSITE & ABOVE: By highlighting the simple architectural detail with color, an extra layer of interest is introduced to the circulation space. Here, a yacht table from Soane and two life buoys from the clients' yacht add to the nautical theme that dominates the rooms of the main floor.

121

ABOVE & OPPOSITE: Campbell's Pamir design, a contemporary take on a classic paisley pattern, dominates this bedroom suite. It brings a freshness to the intimate spaces—on the bedroom walls, the bathroom curtains, and upholstered pieces. The round rattan table in the bathroom is from Soane.

OPPOSITE & ABOVE: In another guest suite, a floor painted with a striking chevron design sets the tone for both the bedroom and the adjoining bathroom. On the bed skirt and chair, a large-scale ikat design complements the look. The dormer windows have fabric-wrapped shutters, which match the curtains and pelmet. All fabrics are from C&C Milano.

ABOVE & OPPOSITE: The striking accent color is made all the more impactful with the dramatic contrast of white walls, tiled floor, and furniture. The room's palette is echoed in the framed works of art, and the giraffe lamp adds a note of whimsy.

ABOVE & OPPOSITE: The changing rooms that serve the pool have a utilitarian but vintage feel thanks to ornithological prints, wall-mounted lanterns, and Shaker-style peg shelves. Simple, horizontal boarding enhances the rustic feel. While the men's changing room (*above*) is trimmed in a darker blue, its feminine counterpart is trimmed in a paler shade (*opposite*).

# THE PLAYHOUSE

For six generations, these three hundred acres of coast have been a world away from everyday life. It is a place that isn't governed by early morning starts, overly burdened schedules, and rigid bedtimes. Instead, one activity flows into another: resting, reading, relaxing, a few hours out on the water, a long lunch with views of the Atlantic. Late starts and afternoon naps that might be unimaginable in any other season become the new norm and lead to even later nights. Where better to spend them than in a nightclub all your own?

The owners of the house are big entertainers, and every effort is made to ensure that lunches, early evening cocktails, dinners, and late-night partying are opportunities for merrymaking. A desire for a building dedicated to entertaining was the premise for the first meeting between Nina Campbell and the clients in Nassau. It was Campbell's role as the driving force behind Annabel's that was the genesis of her long career creating interiors that combine comfort, style, and a playfulness that has made her one of the world's most celebrated designers.

The husband had some ideas he was keen to pursue, notably an entrance that can be opened only by making a call in a London telephone box, the iconic design created by Sir Giles Gilbert Scott based on Sir John Soane's mausoleum at St. Pancras Old Church. The box has been painted in a shade of lavender in line with so many other decorative features in the house. This surreal touch sets the tone for the rest of the space that is

furnished with its own cocktail bar and VIP area, re-creating the look and feel of an elegant city nightclub. Quirky touches abound: notably a standard lamp with a shade made from ostrich feathers, which illuminates a games table and imbues the space with an exotic feel, and gilded mirror panels from Sterling Studios, the London decorative arts company founded by Fiona Sutcliffe and François Lavenir. The inlaid floor juxtaposes woods with different grains to create a discreetly textured feel. Elsewhere, decorative finishes—from the mirrored wall behind the cocktail bar to such subtle architectural details as the gilded ceiling rose—add sophisticated notes to this party villa in the Maine woods.

It is the detailed and subtle layering of the space where the magic lies. A decorative cornice that doubles as a pelmet is backlit with LED lighting that can be changed to a range of different colors to create a look that couldn't be further removed from the rugged simplicity of the New England coast. In the early evening, voile blinds create a soft, diffused light.

Alongside bespoke upholstery, several classic pieces lend gravitas, notably a low table by Maison Baguès—the Parisian furniture firm that collaborated with leading designers of the mid-twentieth century including Maison Jansen, Raymond Subes, and Armand-Albert Rateau—that sits in front of the corner sofa in the VIP area. The particular specialty of Baguès is wrought iron, and this fine example of their work demonstrates the possibilities of the material. The furniture grouping near the fireplace is

PRECEDING SPREAD & OPPOSITE: Landscaping by New York–based garden designer Deborah Nevins has brought the natural world that surrounds the main house right to the doorstep of the Playhouse, in particular a carpet of ferns that abound at the property. Local arborist Tom Savage created the carved panels on the walls of the structure.

135

centered on a table by Belgian sculptor Paula Swinnen, who also creates furniture based on natural forms.

Part of the complex is the bowling alley. Of all the spaces on the property this area does the most to connect with the natural surroundings; beautifully hewn carvings created by local artisans, structural timber in the raw, and hunting trophies create a look and feel that is deeply rooted in the domestic traditions of this part of the world.

The building also has spaces that accommodate more strenuous activities, including a squash court and an exercise room. Upstairs are two guest rooms that are as playful as the nightclub and bowling alley but are more closely related to rooms of traditional Maine cottages:

One is hung with fabric from London-based Chelsea Textiles, another with fabric from Jean Monro, the late, legendary British designer famed for her bold florals. The latter bedroom has a magnificent four-poster—hung with plain white fabric on the outside and the same Jean Monro fabric on the inside—that dominates the space. In the hallway is a wallpaper featuring branches by British designer Juliet Travers that serves as a backdrop for carved-wood trophies of animal heads, which create a quirky sylvan atmosphere. Further embracing this theme, ceramics—including a plate that was the result of a collaboration between the New York designer John Derian and the Parisian ceramic manufacturer Astier de Villatte—are displayed in the bedroom suites.

PRECEDING SPREAD, ABOVE & OPPOSITE: A sculpture by Barry Flanagan creates the central focus of this serene and intimate space, which attracts wildlife and offers a beautiful tableau through the windows of the building.

RIGHT: The lofty proportions of the Playhouse entrance
hall—which is dominated by an oak-leaf chandelier
and wall sconces designed by husband-and-wife team
Christopher and Nicola Cox, founders of Cox London—
add drama to the rustic simplicity of the building.

140

OPPOSITE: A painting of a forest scene is in tune with the acres of spruce trees that surround the building. ABOVE: The Playhouse accommodates more strenuous activities including a squash court and exercise room. Rather than being a purely functional space, the latter has high ceilings and plenty of natural light that create a serene environment.

ABOVE & OPPOSITE: The pared-back feel of the circulation spaces in the building is offset
by such fanciful touches as a candy cart, garden benches painted in vibrant yellow, and
oversize woven-wood urns. Several years ago, the client purchased a door frame, which was
forgotten—it was repurposed as a grand frame for the mirror in this space.

OPPOSITE & ABOVE: While many of the spaces are decorated in a limited palette of paint colors and plain fabrics, there are occasional splashes of pattern, including in the men's changing room where a rich ikat pattern adds an exotic flavor.

PRECEDING SPREAD, OPPOSITE & ABOVE: The viewing space adjacent to the squash court
includes two chairs upholstered in a textile by Kazumi Yoshida, the creative director
of Clarence House in New York. The seat cushions on the L-shaped sofa were upholstered
in plain colors that coordinate with the animated textiles of the chairs and pillows.

151

DESPITE BEING A LEAGUE BOWLER IN THE BIG LEBOWSKI, THE DUDE IS THE ONLY ONE NEVER SEEN BOWLING THROUGHOUT THE MOVIE.

2      1 2 3 4 5 6 7 8 9 10  0:00
Player 1                     0
Player 2                     0
Player 3                     0

*It's how the game is one.*

PRECEDING SPREAD, ABOVE & OPPOSITE: Handcrafted decorative elements and furniture lend a
depth and richness to the bowling alley. Wherever possible, local artisans were employed to create
the bespoke joinery for the storage of such equipment as bowling balls, pins, and shoes. Maine
craftsmen made the carved panels, which run the entire length of the room, above the windows.

PRECEDING SPREAD, OPPOSITE & ABOVE: Among the distinctive pieces in the bowling alley sitting area are a graphic rug from Pierre Frey and sofa tables designed by Rita Konig for The Lacquer Company. Paneled walls and sporting trophies give this room a woodsy atmosphere.

PRECEDING SPREAD, ABOVE & OPPOSITE: Before given entry to the property's private nightclub,
guests are required to dial a secret number in the vintage British telephone booth,
which is painted a striking lavender. Neon lighting lends the space a moody, clubby ambience.

PRECEDING SPREADS, ABOVE & OPPOSITE: Window blinds in a bespoke devoré velvet from Philadelphia-based design studio Kevin O'Brien, a platinum-leafed ceiling, the silvered ceiling rose, and a rug from British designer Luke Irwin add glamour to the nightclub.

170

ABOVE & OPPOSITE: The walls were lacquered by Dean Barger, who was responsible for
many of the decorative paint finishes around the various buildings on the property.
The color of the LED lights recessed under the cornice can be changed to suit the occasion.

OPPOSITE & ABOVE: The attention to detail isn't limited to the decoration of the Playhouse; the building also has a fully stocked bar. During busy times of the year, there is a professional bartender serving family and guests a full complement of drinks and cocktails.

ABOVE & OPPOSITE: In those parts of the house where there is little in the way of decoration, such as this staircase, architectural detail that is simple, elegant, and refined ensures they are more than functional. This window based on a Georgian fanlight is a beautiful example.

176

ABOVE & OPPOSITE: Much of the charm of many of the spaces of the property derives from the contrast between crisp architectural details and the texture of such antique pieces as this highly patinated chest of drawers. This landing leads to the two guest bedroom suites of the Playhouse.

OPPOSITE & ABOVE: The eye is distracted from the sloping angles of this space by a wallpaper on a woodland theme by British designer Juliet Travers. The pattern is complemented by a collection of carved-wood animal trophies that reference the wildlife inhabiting the property.

OPPOSITE & ABOVE: In this striking decorative theme, Sophie's Thistle—a
linen design from the classic British brand Jean Monro—both hangs on the
walls of the entry hallway of a guest bedroom suite and lines the inside of
the bed hangings, while the outside has been faced with plain white linen.

ABOVE & OPPOSITE: Despite their apparent simplicity, the bed hangings have an added
layer of interest thanks to the lacework border that runs down their length and
along the base of the pelmet. A pair of fan-shaped windows flanks the chimney breast.

184

OPPOSITE & ABOVE: A rich palette in the dressing area and bathroom creates a cosseting feel. The trim around the joinery and along the border of the ceiling creates additional detail that enhances the sense that this is a fully resolved space.

187

OPPOSITE & ABOVE: The second bedroom suite has walls hung with Tiny Suzani, a hand-embroidered linen-cotton mix designed by Kit Kemp, the creative force behind some of London's and New York's most stylish hotels.

PRECEDING SPREAD: A dining area furnished with klismos chairs, whose design goes back to ancient Greece, and a rough-hewn fire surround provides a good view of the courtyard garden. ABOVE: A plate designed by London-based artist Florence Houston offers yet another nod to the forest theme. OPPOSITE: Chaise longues on a terrace of the Playhouse offer places to rest and take in the glorious scenery.

# THE LANDSCAPE

Maine has long been a setting for creativity in gardening, perhaps most famously in the hands of Beatrix Farrand, the legendary landscape designer who in the early twentieth century worked her magic at The Eyrie, now the Abby Aldrich Rockefeller Garden at Seal Harbor. Farrand's work offers plenty of inspiration for contemporary designers, particularly in the use of native varieties and naturalistic planting.

Maine's bold, elemental character—the sea, the dramatic coastline, and the forested landscape—demanded a bespoke approach to gardens with a seamless connection between the tamed and the untamed. Deborah Nevins, the New York–based designer who worked on the reinvention of the garden and its surroundings, managed this transition beautifully. At its heart, the woodland is dark and carpeted with moss, but in places it was opened up with the expertise of late arborist Thomas Savage to create paths and areas for clay pigeon shooting. A mixture of birch and such native plants as sweet gale, winterberry, and bayberry was planted to soften the transition between the domestic and the wild. In addition, rhododendrons that had to be moved when the house was rebuilt were reinstated.

The fact that there was a symbiotic relationship between the house and its setting is thanks to Nevins's involvement from the outset and her careful stewardship of the gardens and grounds. Because the living accommodation is divided between a number of different outbuildings—notably the pool house and the Playhouse but also garages and other ancillary structures—the property required a master plan that created not just coherence but also easy and pleasant transition from one building to the other. One of the most striking examples of this is the vaulted pergola that joins the main house to the pool house. The hard landscaping plays an important part in this connection, and in many places it lends color and texture with beautiful stones, in particular Roxbury granite that is quarried in Connecticut and that was used in the construction of New York's Grand Central Terminal and Brooklyn Bridge.

This is a landscape that is about more than just long views and sweeping vistas. Like so much about this house and its surroundings, it has, for six generations, been a place to entertain family and friends. Dotted around the property are settings for lunches, dinners, and drinks that add yet more dimension to the multitude of entertaining opportunities on offer. It is a productive garden, too, with a vegetable garden given a rustic feel by woven hurdles made locally. Where possible, Nevins sourced from artisans in the surrounding area; among others she worked with Lunaform, the pottery studio in Maine that supplies pots and tabletops, some of which have been imprinted with ferns that are such a ubiquitous feature of the area and which imbue the garden with a distinctive sense of place.

OPPOSITE: Maine's craggy coastline boasts a proud maritime tradition dating back centuries. In summer, it's a popular destination for pleasure cruisers who come to explore its remote coves and fishing villages. The owners of the property have their own boat that they use to explore the surrounding area. FOLLOWING SPREADS: Coastal views, including the back facade of the house, from the water. The dock is a perfect setting for a leisurely lunch.

ABOVE & OPPOSITE: A magnificent porte cochere—popular in the eighteenth and nineteenth centuries to protect arriving and departing guests—connects the main entrance court to a side entrance of the house and garaging. Designed in the local vernacular, it blends seamlessly with the architecture of the main house and connects to the grand garden trellis beyond.
FOLLOWING SPREADS: The abundant gardens provide food for the table and a feast for the eyes.

OPPOSITE & ABOVE: Just as the main house, the Playhouse, and the pool house offer plenty of settings for entertaining, so does the garden. This terrace hidden away from the main house is furnished with rustic furniture that reflects the sylvan context of the property—perfect for an early summer lunch or afternoon tea.

ABOVE & OPPOSITE: Wherever possible, the landscape designer worked with local artisans on design elements of the garden. In the kitchen garden woven wattle has been used to create borders in the plots dedicated to the vegetables and herbs that supply the kitchen. FOLLOWING SPREAD: The garden is an environment of constant stimulation with seasonal flowers; insects, including glorious butterflies; and a frog, who became a friend of Campbell's during her many visits.

OPPOSITE & ABOVE: The aim of landscape designer Deborah Nevins was to create a seamless connection
between the manipulated environment and its natural setting. Here, Tom Savage's masterfully
carved gate leads you into the woods, after you have had a drink from a conveniently positioned "bar."

PRECEDING SPREAD, ABOVE & OPPOSITE: The magnificent tennis pavilion combines two local building materials—cedar shingles and rough stone—to create a look that is perfectly in keeping with the setting. FOLLOWING SPREAD: A food truck, here decorated for a Mexican-themed party, is a perfect movable source of entertainment with food and drink. On this occasion, the festivities were moved indoors to a capacious storeroom due to a sudden Maine rainstorm!

ABOVE, OPPOSITE & FOLLOWING SPREAD: In addition to the multitude of settings
for entertaining around the property, there is a tent that is erected for
Moroccan-themed dinners. The dramatic sky at dusk and the lapping of the
waves at the shoreline are a peaceful backdrop when socializing outdoors.

ABOVE, OPPOSITE & FOLLOWING SPREADS: When Campbell's clients took ownership of the property, they worked with local arborist Tom Savage. The woodland that was untouched for decades was opened up and such native trees as sweet gale, winterberry, and bayberry were reintroduced to create a softer transition from cultivated garden to woodland. A greenhouse is the perfect setting for an autumnal meal.

ABOVE, OPPOSITE & FOLLOWING SPREAD: When creating the wide range of spaces around the property, care was taken to ensure that there were rooms suited to seasons other than summer. Paddle tennis can be played in the colder months, and Campbell created an intimate setting to watch the sport as well as to socialize over food and drinks by a warming fire.

# ACKNOWLEDGMENTS

I feel very lucky to have been involved with this project, which is one of my most exciting to date. The property owners, my wonderful clients, created a "dream team" right from the start. I would firstly like to thank those clients and their house team for their immeasurable patience.

It was an absolute delight to work with the inspired architects at Ferguson & Shamamian, especially my day-to-day interactions with Scott Sottile and Sole Mendez.

Nate Holyoke and his extraordinary building company made everything I suggested a reality—and with a positive attitude!

Debbie Nevins and her team masterminded the most exquisite landscaping and gardens.

Shashi Caudill was a big asset with the art advisory.

All of my team at Nina Campbell Ltd. endlessly supported me with their hard work.

Paul Raeside perfectly captured the essence of the property with his beautiful photographs.

A special thank-you to my daughter Alice Sharples: her stylish eye and fabulous humor made photographing the images for this book a wonderful experience.

I additionally acknowledge Giles Kime for writing the book with me; Philip Reeser and all at Rizzoli for editing and producing the work; and Doug Turshen and Steve Turner for designing the book.

I particularly note Tom Savage, a wonderful local arborist we worked with and who very sadly passed away soon after the project was completed.

This whole property has a wonderful feel created with good humor and good tempers and was so much fun to accomplish, which I think now shows in the soul of this home by the sea.    —*Nina Campbell*

First published in the United States of America in 2023 by
Rizzoli International Publications, Inc.
300 Park Avenue South
New York, New York 10010
rizzoliusa.com

Publisher: Charles Miers
Senior Editor: Philip Reeser
Production Manager: Barbara Sadick
Design Coordinator: Olivia Russin
Copy Editor: Claudia Bauer
Proofreader: Sarah Stump
Managing Editor: Lynn Scrabis

Designer: Doug Turshen with Steve Turner

ISBN: 978-0-8478-9909-8
Library of Congress Control Number: 2022941764

2023 2024 2025 2026 / 10 9 8 7 6 5 4 3 2 1

Printed in Singapore

Facebook.com/RizzoliNewYork
Twitter: @Rizzoli_Books
Instagram.com/RizzoliBooks
Pinterest.com/RizzoliBooks
Youtube.com/user/RizzoliNY
Issuu.com/Rizzoli